I Choose, He Gives

From His Heart to Yours

JUDE WAY

Trilogy Christian Publishers

A Wholly Owned Subsidiary of Trinity Broadcasting Network

2442 Michelle Drive | Tustin, CA 92780

Copyright © 2024 by Judith L. Way

All Scripture quotations, unless otherwise noted, are taken from THE HOLY BIBLE, NEW INTERNATIONAL VERSION®, NIV® Copyright © 1973, 1978, 1984, 2011 by Biblica, Inc.® Used by permission. All rights reserved worldwide.

Scripture quotations marked ESV are taken from the ESV® Bible (The Holy Bible, English Standard Version®), copyright © 2001 by Crossway Bibles, a publishing ministry of Good News Publishers. Used by permission. All rights reserved.

All rights reserved, including the right to reproduce this book or portions thereof in any form whatsoever.

For information, address Trilogy Christian Publishing

Rights Department, 2442 Michelle Drive, Tustin, CA 92780.

Trilogy Christian Publishing/ TBN and colophon are trademarks of Trinity Broadcasting Network.

For information about special discounts for bulk purchases, please contact Trilogy Christian Publishing.

Trilogy Disclaimer: The views and content expressed in this book are those of the author and may not necessarily reflect the views and doctrine of Trilogy Christian Publishing or the Trinity Broadcasting Network.

10 9 8 7 6 5 4 3 2 1

Library of Congress Cataloging-in-Publication Data is available.

ISBN 979-8-89597-098-0

ISBN 979-8-89597-099-7

TABLE OF CONTENTS

Meet Jude 5

Let's Get Started 7

Daily Living 9

Peace and Joy 49

Suffering 92

Prayer 128

Forgiveness 158

Final Thoughts 181

Acknowledgments. .183

Endnotes 185

MEET JUDE

It was the winter of 1945 deep in enemy territory of WWII Germany when Ernie Hodge's squad came under attack. He would be the only U.S. soldier to survive. In 1946 that man became Jude's daddy.

Born and raised in Cincinnati, Ohio, to Ernie and Alma Hodge, Jude spent her childhood learning about the Lord at Springdale Nazarene Church. The Lord quickly became the center of her heart.

Jude and her husband, Tony Way, have shared a remarkable life. Starting a post-college career as youth pastors, their entire marriage has involved ministering to young lives. From children's ministry to teen ministry, speaking at conferences all over the country, and teaching and mentoring young couples, they have always served wherever the Lord needed them.

A lot of the people they've met along the way are still in Tony and Jude's life; some even as long as fifty years, including some of the children/teens from early on.

Professionally, Jude became a successful actress, landing multiple roles for both commercial films and print advertisements. With her success, she started a business to train actors and actresses.

While acting was fulfilling, the call for Jude's life was counseling new Christians and those in times of strife.

It is no exaggeration to say that she has touched the lives of hundreds, maybe even thousands, of people, lovingly coaching but always leading them back to Jesus.

LET'S GET STARTED

Every morning, I pray and ask God to give me a scripture for the day. This book contains many of those scriptures/messages. They are arranged by topic, so feel free to open a page at random or to use sequentially. Trust that God will speak to give you encouragement, affirmation, courage, and counsel for what you need today and in this moment... *May each one bless you as they have me!*

"I choose, He gives" is a phrase God gave me in 1999, in the middle of the night during a season of stress when I couldn't sleep.

I realized the only way He could bless me as much as He wanted was to choose His control over my situation and my life, not my own, each and every day.

What are you choosing today—His way or your way? Are you choosing His thoughts, or are you dwelling on what you think, see, or know? Thankfully, when we choose Him, we KNOW we will be just fine!

DAILY LIVING

So many of us are hard on ourselves because we just don't feel like we can be perfect enough to serve the Lord. When we remember each day to give up our will and replace it with God's will, we learn to love Him more than ourselves. Ironically, this helps us learn to love ourselves better.

In the book of Matthew 22:34–40 (ESV), Jesus says,

> But when the Pharisees heard that he had silenced the Sadducees, they gathered together. And one of them, a lawyer, asked him a question to test him. "Teacher, which is the great commandment in the Law?" And he said to him, "You shall love the Lord your God with all your heart and with all your soul and with all your mind. This is the great and first commandment. And a second is like it: You shall love your neighbor as yourself. On these two commandments depend all the Law and the Prophets."

Love is the keyword here. God is love, and He wants us to love ourselves and love each other.

Daily Living Day One

"Be alert and of sober mind. Your enemy the devil prowls around like a roaring lion looking for someone to devour" (1 Peter 5:8).

When you feel yourself attacked repeatedly, that's a sign that God is about to do something amazing in your life and the devil is trying to get in His way. When you read the scripture above, notice the phrase—*devil as like a lion*—but he's not a lion; it's all an act. The devil is weaker than God! God's plan is more powerful than anything the devil can throw at you. Saturate your life with God's Word, pray to stay within His will; then wait and watch God go to work. He can use all things for good according to his will. Take refuge from the storms of life in His Word; let it surround and provide you comfort while you wait.

Daily Living Day Two

"Ascribe to the Lord the glory due his name; bring an offering and come before him. Worship the Lord in the splendor of his holiness" (1 Chronicles 16:29).

Over the years I have created a weekly routine for household chores. Thursdays became my busy day: changing sheets, doing laundry, and getting groceries. A friend told me a long time ago to put worship music on during the tedious times of life. Put it on in the car, and loud; put it on louder than the sound of the dishwasher or the laundry machines. Welcome the Holy Spirit into your tedious times and allow Him to bless you. I always say there is only one thing better than the visitation of the Holy Spirit...another one! Hallelujah!

Daily Living Day Three

"*It always protects, always trusts, always hopes, always perseveres*" *(1 Corinthians 13:7).*

We know that Jesus forgave the soldiers who nailed Him to the Cross. He told His mother Mary that John the disciple was now her son and that she was now John's mother. Jesus took care of it all while He was suffering. He was still following His Father's plans. Sometimes, even when we're suffering, we have to continue to do His will. Jesus didn't act from what He saw or what He felt. He acted from the love of His Father living inside His heart. An unconditional, powerful life of love. An opportunity to show others a faith that will not waver. That's what He wants us to choose!

Daily Living Day Four

"Now to him who is able to do immeasurably more than all we ask or imagine, according to his power that is at work within us" (Ephesians 3:20).

You know who you are and you know where you are, but more importantly, Jesus does too! The past, the present, and the future are all one day to Him! He has all power over Heaven and Earth. He can and will take care of all things. Let Him!

Daily Living Day Five

"So that Christ may dwell in your hearts through faith. And I pray that you, being rooted and established in love" (Ephesians 3:17).

Are you blooming? I'm not referring to the old saying, "Bloom where you are planted." That always makes me think I'm being directed to dig in my heels right where I am, make the best of my situation, and do good things with what I have.

That's okay in some situations, but that's not what I mean by blooming. In order for a flower to grow and bloom, opening up its delicate petals, it must be rooted in good, rich soil.

It becomes something so beautiful that you can't take your eyes off of it. When the Holy Spirit dwells within us, we're rooted and grounded in the deepest, richest life-giving nourishment we could ever have. Let him fill you and lead you so you can bloom as beautifully as He intends.

Daily Living Day Six

"Therefore, if anyone is in Christ, the new creation has come: the old has gone, the new is here!" (2 Corinthians 5:17).

While praying for a friend and their children, I made a comment in a way that I had never made before. Often, I have said that a child is a clean slate; everyone that comes into their life will have an entry written on the slate that will impact them. Being a trained actress, I can recall how a scene or a commercial is made. Often, when you go on a set they hand you what is called a storyboard. It looks like a comic strip in the paper. It shows you how every scene and dialogue is going to happen. You get that in your head, then act it out!

A child's slate is like those storyboards. Does their "acting" depict them leading the life God wants for them? If not, ask God, "Lord, erase the storyboard that has been written throughout their lives. Replace it with who Jesus is and His plan for them. Change their way of thinking, Lord, about themselves and others." Each of us has our own storyboard! Let's give it to Jesus to erase, remake, and control our lives! Praise His Holy Name! I choose, He gives.

Daily Living Day Seven

"But those who hope in the Lord will renew their strength. They will soar on wings like eagles; they will run and not grow weary; they will walk and not be faint" (Isaiah 40:31).

Yesterday I was walking past my window and I saw these large leaves floating on by. They looked free and gentle and beautiful. I wondered how they could float so easily. I concluded it's because they are light and nothing is weighing them down.

Then suddenly I thought...what if we could cast off of us the things that weigh us down: past memories, fears of tomorrow, worries about getting everything done that needs to be done?

If we could lay everything down in front of Jesus, just think how we would soar through life. We would have the freedom to do the things that He wants us to do. Our relationships would be healthier; our hearts would have so much love, joy, and peace.

Try this: picture yourself as a large leaf gently floating through the air and Jesus is the wind beneath your wings.

Daily Living Day Eight

"For I know the plans I have for you," declares the Lord, "plans to prosper you and not to harm you, plans to give you hope and a future" (Jeremiah 29:11).

To live life with a true purpose is to walk in peace!

Searching for that purpose sometimes creates frustration.

Praying and believing in purpose gives us God's power and wisdom, not just our limited vision.

As I spoke with a friend of fifty-plus years, I realized she and I have lived by God's power and have each lived our lives with His purpose guiding us.

As young girls we wanted to be women of strength and faith!

Living with thankful hearts and always looking to His story, we managed to avoid countless frustrations and, in the process, discovered His unique purpose for each of our lives. Are you focusing on His story, the world's story, or your own?

Daily Living Day Nine

"A new command I give you: Love one another. As I have loved you, so you must love one another" (John 13:34).

Have you ever had an instant connection with someone? You just knew you would do anything in the world for them.

When your eyes met and they smiled back, your souls connected. This is how Jesus feels about you; He did everything for you!

The bond you have with Him will heal and strengthen you. Do you need to be reminded of that bond today? The more time you spend with Him and in His presence, the stronger you will know and feel His power in your life!

Daily Living Day Ten

"However, as it is written: 'What no eye has seen, what no ear has heard, and what no human mind has conceived the things God has prepared for those who love him'" (1 Corinthians 2:9).

I have seen God give so many people everything good (even in spite of themselves sometimes), but instead of living in God's will with a thankful heart, they chose what they wanted, thinking it was better. It always ends up in chaos for them until they change their perspective and then choose to live according to His will. Reminds me of someone else...Adam and Eve—you know how that story ended!

Daily Living Day Eleven

"I am not saying this because I am in need, for I have learned to be content whatever the circumstances" (Philippians 4:11).

There are not many times in our lives that we say, "I have too much time on my hands." But if that time ever comes, and some of us are experiencing them now, I think we will find out who we really are. I have experienced those times in my life many times due to health issues since I was ten years old. So, I knew I could adjust once again since I have Jesus. You see, Jesus fills the corners of our hearts like no one and nothing else can.

Daily Living Day Twelve

"Now faith is confidence in what we hope for and assurance about what we do not see" (Hebrews 11:1).

Faith is the substance of things hoped for and the evidence of things not seen.

Dear Lord,

IN FAITH, I give You the difficult times. IN FAITH, I give You the most joy-filled times. IN FAITH, I give You the unknown tomorrow. IN FAITH, I give You my family and friends. IN FAITH, I give you my health IN FAITH, I give you everything BECAUSE OF WHO YOU ARE! Amen

So when the days get hard, just go and worship Him. Turn on worship music, pray for those you love and even those you may not know—someone, somewhere, needs your prayers today. Yes, it's hard staying in the house and not getting the things done we want, but who we are is really who Jesus makes us to be. He makes it all worthwhile. He makes it all make sense. And He gives joy when there seemingly is none.

Daily Living
Day Thirteen

"*My command is this: Love each other as I have loved you*" (John 15:12).

We feed our neighborhood birds and squirrels and regularly see interesting sights, but today I saw something I have only seen three times in the last thirteen months. A male cardinal came over, picked up food from our feeder, flew all the way over to the table on our patio, and fed it to his wife, a female cardinal. It was so sweet and gentle. We saw this gesture for the first time the day my husband came home from his lung rehab and was feeling a little weary. Today, we have been choosing so much hope for our future. I thought of how Tony and I serve each other as husband and wife. As he navigates health challenges, it is now my turn to care for him, and I count that a privilege. Who can you serve today: Jesus, your mate/partner, a friend, or maybe even yourself?

Daily Living
Day Fourteen

"Finally, be strong in the Lord and in his mighty power. Put on the full armor of God, so that you can take your stand against the devil's schemes" (Ephesians 6:10–11).

Grab your lunches, grab your coats, start your cars, and start the running of the week...Oh, WAIT! Did you cover your heart and mind with His armor and His Word? Put on daily the armor of God, choose His sweet Spirit, love those who hurt you, give grace when it is unearned!

Ask the Holy Spirit to give you His hope and His dreams for your day, your week, your life. Lay your head on the shoulder of the One who is the lifter of your head—then SOAR!

He has driven me away and made me walk in darkness rather than light; indeed, he has turned his hand against me again and again, all day long.

Daily Living
Day Fifteen

"He has made my skin and my flesh grow old and has broken my bones. He has besieged me and surrounded me with bitterness and hardship" (Lamentations 3:2–5).

Are you in a place of waiting on God to get you UNSTUCK?

Maybe you aren't stuck at all; maybe you are in a place of learning and preparation to do His perfect will. Not just His permissive will, but His perfect plan for what will be the next season of your life. While we are waiting, He is working, so choose to rest in Him. Listen and learn. Just be in love with Him and trust that peace will come.

Daily Living Day Sixteen

"Keep this Book of the Law always on your lips; meditate on it day and night, so that you may be careful to do everything written in it. Then you will be prosperous and successful" (Joshua 1:8).

On your next weekend, when you have a little more time than during the jam-packed week, I have something BIG I want you to think about.

Yesterday I wanted God's Word in my heart, so I opened it up to a random page. When I looked down, it was a scripture that I hadn't read in twenty years! I didn't think that was possible; I thought I had gone through the whole Bible again since then.

Wow, never doubt His Word is the living Word of God! I knew it had been twenty years because of the date and notes I had written beside it. I'm not going to tell you what it was because I want you to try it yourself. Do what Jesus' mother Mary did and "ponder it in your heart" The scripture I am referring to spoke so deeply to me. Read your scripture and think about it for the next two days. What have you been pondering—hurt, unforgiveness, anger, discontentment, fear, pain of some kind, finances, sin, emotions? Instead, ponder on God's Word and His Love!

DAILY LIVING
DAY SEVENTEEN

"I am not saying this because I am in need, for I have learned to be content whatever the circumstances" (Philippians 4:11).

Often those of us with big personalities jump in full force before a situation is fully known. The wonderful part about that is that God understands. He didn't condemn the biblical zealots who were impulsive but redirected them with His love.

He understood Peter, who was outspoken, and sometimes not in a good way.

He understood Zacchaeus when he ran up to the top of a tree to see above the crowd gathered as Jesus passed by. Jesus just said to him, "Zacchaeus, you come down, for I'm going to your house today."

Though there are undoubtedly things about each of us we don't like, everything about us is beautiful to the Lord because He made us this way.

Dear Lord, today use me with all my personality—for Your glory. Help me not to be anything other than who You made me to be.

Daily Living
Day Eighteen

"That person should not expect to receive anything from the Lord. Such a person is double-minded and unstable in all they do" (James 1:7–8).

When awarding the Medal of Honor, the President used the term "larger than life" in speaking of this soldier. It made me think about how large life can be. We just have to be bigger than the circumstances in this demanding life. But how? It really comes from our resolve to do what is right regardless of the cost—also known as integrity! Matthew says, "Where your treasure is, there your heart will be also."

It is so much easier to make a courageous choice when your mind has chosen what or who you treasure most. This is why I call my Christian walk a love affair with Jesus. I love Jesus and will never purposely do anything to hurt Him or to misrepresent Him. Doesn't mean I don't make mistakes, but it's never intentional. In my mind Jesus is my one true love.

For every great decision that requires courage, I judge by who He is, not by who I am. The Bible says, "A double-minded man is unstable in all they do." We will never be perfect like our Savior, but it can always and should be our sole goal to keep our focus on Jesus and His teachings. It helps keep the tough days not so messy. What does He give? Life more abundant.

Daily Living
Day Nineteen

"But seek first his kingdom and his righteousness, and all these things will be given to you as well" (Matthew 6:33).

When everyone begins to think about a new year approaching, they usually make a "New Year's resolution." If Jesus were sitting in the room with us right now, He'd tell us what we need is a new heart. Everything starts from the heart. God gave Moses a list of ten things (also known as the 10 Commandments), which was a Do Not Do list. Jesus came to us to show us how to live so that our hearts are changed, causing us to want to/choose to keep those commandments. Choose to love Jesus more than anything. He will change your heart and take care of everything else! "Seek ye first the Kingdom of God and all these things will be added to you!"

Daily Living Day Twenty

"So we fix our eyes not on what is seen, but on what is unseen, since what is seen is temporary, but what is unseen is eternal" (2 Corinthians 4:18).

Remember whenever you spend time with many different people, we often judge or are judged by our attitude and perspective. Ask Jesus to help you see things through His eyes. Those are eyes of grace and mercy. Remember, no one defines us; the only one that matters is Jesus! Thank You, Jesus, for coming to earth to show us how to live!

Daily Living
Day Twenty-One

"Do not be anxious about anything, but in every situation, by prayer and petition, with thanksgiving, present your requests to God. 7 And the peace of God, which transcends all understanding, will guard your hearts and your minds in Christ Jesus" (Philippians 4:6–7).

I love the word THANKSGIVING. Thanks and giving are great as two words. We give thanks for the things in our lives, our homes, our family, our friends, and most importantly, our God!

If people can see us live with a thankful heart, it will enhance any relationship we have and even the relationships of those we love. We can give others a look at who Jesus is when they see how the Holy Spirit can lift us in all our circumstances. Remember what I told you about the series *Veggie Tales*? The message of one episode says, "A thankful heart is a happy heart."

Daily Living
Day Twenty-Two

"In addition to all this, take up the shield of faith, with which you can extinguish all the flaming arrows of the evil one" (Ephesians 6:16).

Dear Lord, as we start each new day or a new week, we ask for Your wisdom, courage, and joy. As we put on Your armor and the shield of faith, we are reminded that You protect us not only from others but also from ourselves.

The Bible says that "faith is the substance of things hoped for, the evidence of things not seen." We are reminded to trust You for what we don't see and have hope. Holy Spirit, may we all rest in Your care.

Daily Living
Day Twenty-Three

"The name of the Lord is a fortified tower; the righteous run to it and are safe" (Proverbs 18:10).

Last weekend when we were shopping with our grandchildren, the youngest one, a teenager, kept taking my hand as we walked. I was so touched. It was like she was saying, I am thankful for you. I need you for my safety... you have my heart! So today I am reaching out for my Savior's hand! Walking through life holding His hand because I'm thankful for Him, and I need Him for my safety. He has my heart!

DAILY LIVING
DAY TWENTY-FOUR

"Trust in the Lord with all your heart and lean not on your own understanding; in all your ways submit to him, and he will make your paths straight" (PROVERBS 3:5–6).

Well, you made it! Don't let the devil whisper the wrong things in your ears. Stay as close to the Lord as you can so Satan doesn't have access to who you are and where you're headed in your life! "Trust in the Lord, with all your heart, lean, not upon your own understanding in all your ways, acknowledge him, and he will direct your path."

DAILY LIVING
DAY TWENTY-FIVE

"I seek you with all my heart; do not let me stray from your commands" (Psalms 119:10).

Great peace has those who love Thy Word and nothing will offend them. I've given you this scripture before, but it came to me so clearly that each of us needs to be reminded that temptations of this world can creep in so quickly. The more we commune with God, praying, reading His Word, and listening to Him, the quicker will be your ability to turn to the Holy Spirit! We will be able to identify when Satan is whispering to us and what is coming from the Lord. Like any other skill, the more we practice the quicker Satan is cut off!! Thank You, Jesus, for giving us this ability just by loving and listening to You! Let us walk by faith.

Daily Living
Day Twenty-Six

"I pray that out of his glorious riches he may strengthen you with power through his Spirit in your inner being" (Ephesians 3:16).

Have you ever heard someone say, "That's just the way I am"? In other words, you have accepted my behavior no matter what because that's who I am. Despite our flaws, Jesus loves us as we are and wants us to be the best version of ourselves. In the Bible God tells us: 1. We are fearfully and wonderfully made. 2. Love as I have loved you. 3. Your life bears good fruit... love, joy, peace, long suffering, gentleness, goodness, kindness, meekness, and self-control. When we have the mind of Christ our behavior changes. Whether you have uttered those words or heard them from someone else, remember you don't have to stay where you are, as you are. God wants to give blessings beyond our imagination; we just have to receive them.

DAILY LIVING
DAY TWENTY-SEVEN

"Whatever you have learned or received or heard from me, or seen in me—put it into practice. And the God of peace will be with you" (Philippians 4:9).

"Don't judge yourself or others, just learn!" This was a common theme in messages to singles Bible study groups. Learn your lesson well, my friend, learn your lesson well! Simple, right? Jesus wanted to speak His lessons to us clearly in ways we could understand.

I think that's why He spoke in parables. He knew a story wouldn't burden us with guilt weighing us down but would allow us to receive the lesson and grow.

"Whatever you have learned or received from or heard from me or have seen in me, put it into practice and the God of peace will be with you."

Daily Living
Day Twenty-Eight

"You make known to me the path of life; you will fill me with joy in your presence, with eternal pleasures at your right hand" (Psalms 16:11).

There's an old song, "I walked today where Jesus walked." The best advice I can give to you today is to walk in His steps. Don't walk ahead of Him and be afraid, walk behind Him and let Him show you the path.

Daily Living
Day Twenty-Nine

"Here I am! I stand at the door and knock. If anyone hears my voice and opens the door, I will come in and eat with that person, and they with me" (Revelation 3:20).

Think about this before you start your day or week: how do I handle the chaos and pace of daily life? Something I've said many times—talk to Jesus when you are chasing after your job, ministry, groceries, and yes, your kids! Talk to Him; when He is needed the most He will be there. May He fill you with His Holy Presence before, during, and continually in your day.

Daily Living
Day Thirty

"Let him lead me to the banquet hall, and let his banner over me be love" (Song of Solomon 2:4).

Come sit at His table. Have you heard this phrase before? A dining room table is a place not only to share a meal but also a time to share our lives with each other. Pull up a chair to the Holy Spirit's table. Listen to the Holy Spirit's message. We need God's perspective to guide us each day.

Daily Living
Day Thirty-One

"I press on toward the goal to win the prize for which God has called me heavenward in Christ Jesus" (Philippians 3:14).

Dear Lord, we give You this day and every day. Help us to see it all through Your eyes and give us the strength to push above circumstances that are keeping us from doing what You've called us to do. Is there something in your life you keep putting off? I can think of several things in my own life. What are yours?

Daily Living
Day Thirty-Two

"God is within her, she will not fall; God will help her at break of day" (Psalms 46:5).

Good morning. Whatever You have for me today and whatever this week has for me, I will face it with strength, courage, joy, laughter, and peace. Not because of who I am or who the people are around me, but because of who GOD is. He is never failing, always ready to give me all I need to handle anything I'll face. He is my first love, and as long as I keep Him first in all my decisions in life, my family and I will be victors!

Daily Living
Day Thirty-Three

"He says, 'Be still, and know that I am God; I will be exalted among the nations, I will be exalted in the earth'" (Psalms 46:10).

Simple moments in life make everything easier! Finding such joy in something as simple as our Christmas tree. When our girls were little, we would turn off the room's lights and lay under the tree and I would read to them. Forget Instagram, Pinterest, Facebook, and your phone camera. Instead, just be in the moment. Be present and enjoy those small moments! Rest for the soul is often found in quiet, uncomplicated places!

Daily Living
Day Thirty-Four

"However, as it is written: 'What no eye has seen, what no ear has heard, and what no human mind has conceived" — the things God has prepared for those who love him—'" (1 Corinthians 2:9).

I have seen God give so many people everything good (even in spite of themselves sometimes), but instead of living in God's will with a thankful heart, they chose what they wanted, thinking it was better. It always ends up in chaos for them until they change their perspective and then choose to live according to His will. Reminds me of someone else... Adam and Eve—you know how that story ended!

Daily Living
Day Thirty-Five

"In all your ways submit to him, and he will make your paths straight" (Proverbs 3:6).

Dear Lord, here we are another day to live not only for You but live like You! We choose again to not look at anything or anyone that defines our day but You! We choose Your eyes to see through. We choose Your heart to love others! We choose Your peace in the midst of this broken world!

Daily Living Day Thirty-Six

"I will give you a new heart and put a new spirit in you; I will remove from you your heart of stone and give you a heart of flesh" (Ezekiel 36:26).

Years ago, when my girls were in college, I was a nanny. One day I heard the parent say to their child, "You aren't being a good family citizen." If we don't teach our children how to function well in the small community of the home, how can they function in the larger community of the world? So now you see one of the reasons why our world is in trouble!

Unless we change our behavior, nothing can change! And behavior only changes if hearts and minds change. Our actions are a window to the heart, so when Jesus looks through the window of your heart, what will He see?

PEACE AND JOY

I do my best not to even get out of bed in the morning without putting on the armor of God. I follow this order: I put on the helmet of salvation, the breastplate of righteousness, the shield of faith, and the sword of His Word, which is the Holy Spirit.

I ask Him to fill me with the Holy Spirit and cover me with His protection. I ask for His Joy and Peace to guide my steps.

Real, perfect peace in the midst of life's difficulties can only come from Him because He can do the supernatural.

Joy is not happiness; happiness is dependent on circumstances and can change constantly. However, Joy is rooted deep in your soul, unaffected by external circumstances. During my husband's six-year cancer battle, I experienced it daily.

God granted me Joy regardless of the situation. He provided me with wisdom that brought peace. Therefore, I chose laughter whenever possible and worshiped Him in my soul, regardless of life's challenges. He holds power and authority over our lives, which should bring us Joy and Peace. Worship transports me emotionally to a different place where peace and joy settle in as I worship Him.

Peace and Joy Day One

"How beautiful on the mountains are the feet of those who bring good news, who proclaim peace, who bring good tidings, who proclaim salvation, who say to Zion, 'Your God reigns!'" (Isaiah 52:7).

The Lord tells us to have our feet fitted with the readiness that comes from the gospel of peace. When we are prepared with God's words and are close to His presence, then we are ready for anything that may come our way; peace comes from that. A warrior is someone who is ready to serve their leader, trusting their leader, believing their leader, and doing whatever they are asked to do—none of which is possible unless they know the heart of their leader. If Jesus is your leader, you have to communicate with and listen to Him in order to know His heart for you.

PEACE AND JOY DAY TWO

"Command and teach these things. Don't let anyone look down on you because you are young, but set an example for the believers in speech, in conduct, in love, in faith and in purity" (Timothy 4:11–12).

Are you burdened by your daily guilt, disappointments, unfulfilled dreams, or weaknesses? When we look at children we see the empty pages of their life story. Teach them wisdom, courage, and love for Jesus! Look, there are many around you ready to learn from your life story. Make it all count by giving away your wisdom, newly reclaimed joy, and yes—even your failures. Jesus changes us to not only a life of peace but a life of purpose.

Peace and Joy Day Three

"But the fruit of the Spirit is love, joy, peace, forbearance, kindness, goodness, faithfulness" (Galatians 5:22).

"But the fruit of the Spirit is love, joy, peace, forgiveness, kindness, goodness and self-control." This is a chapter of freedom! For when we bear the fruit of our choices to live like this, we have true freedom. When we aren't living like this, our lives produce just the opposite. Christians often forget this. Each of us has times when we don't measure up. However, the more we saturate our lives with him, i.e. living in the Spirit, the less we allow our humanness to be in control. In choosing Him, you will find less stress and more peace.

Peace and Joy Day Four

Therefore, since we are surrounded by such a great cloud of witnesses, let us throw off everything that hinders and the sin that so easily entangles. And let us run with perseverance the race marked out for us, fixing our eyes on Jesus, the pioneer and perfecter of faith. For the joy set before him he endured the cross, scorning its shame, and sat down at the right hand of the throne of God. (Hebrews 12:1–2)

I woke up at two o'clock this morning thinking about the clutter in my closet, and I needed to get that stuff out of there. Then I felt like I heard this: What other clutter is in your life that keeps you from being as effective as you should be each day? What is the clutter in your life—is it negativity, a critical spirit, too much busyness, or working too hard? I'm asking the Lord to help me clean out any clutter that might be in my heart and mind! Nothing is more important to me than His presence and power in my life.

I don't know about you, but we just can't survive in this broken world without Him. While I felt frustrated by things beyond my control, I still had joy in several conversations that day. Just think how much more joy I could have had if I had gotten rid of all that unnecessary stuff.

Peace and Joy Day Five

"Be kind and compassionate to one another, forgiving each other, just as in Christ God forgave you" (Ephesians 4:32).

We have to realize when dealing with people of any age, we cannot be their protectors. We are only to love them. Our opinions about truth and wisdom are just that—ours—not theirs or God's and may or may not be welcomed. Trust and respect cannot be forced on anyone. It is earned, and even when it's been earned, they may choose to ignore our words. I counsel so many people about this; someone might need a reminder today. So then what? A reminder...when you have a choice between being right or being kind, choose kindness. Because kindness grows love. Love brings us peace and joy.

Peace and Joy Day Six

"Devote yourselves to prayer, being watchful and thankful" (Colossians 4:2).

Do you find yourself becoming anxious for the "big events" in our daily lives? Making lists and schedules will help, but to ensure you enjoy the event, plan to be done with all the business several days in advance. This not only will calm you down and allow more enjoyment for you, but will bring peace to your home.

PEACE AND JOY DAY SEVEN

"Since, then, you have been raised with Christ, set your hearts on things above, where Christ is, seated at the right hand of God. Set your minds on things above, not on earthly things" (Colossians 3:1–2).

As you start a new season of life, think of these three things: 1. With what do you fill your life? That answer will determine what you will become. 2. Strive to show God's unconditional love to those in your everyday life. 3. Remove whatever or whomever robs you of joy. Don't revisit or go someplace you don't want to stay! These three things will change your reactions to life, which will bring you more peace and joy! That's just who Jesus is! He is in control if you let Him!

Peace and Joy Day Eight

"Therefore if you have any encouragement from being united with Christ, if any comfort from his love, if any common sharing in the Spirit, if any tenderness and compassion, then make my joy complete by being like-minded, having the same love, being one in spirit and of one mind" (Philippians 2:1–2).

We all have days when we feel empty, maybe even a little down. I believe we have those days for a reason. Sometimes it may be from our own choices or the choices of others. But what is important is that we don't just sit in it. It is also healthy to be honest with yourself. So, how should you choose to react on those days? Will you resent those feelings and be even more miserable, or will you learn from them?

Look for purpose, laughter, and opportunities to give love and life to others. You will be surprised how much more peace you will have!

Peace and Joy Day Nine

"Therefore, I urge you, brothers and sisters, in view of God's mercy, to offer your bodies as a living sacrifice, holy and pleasing to God—this is your true and proper worship" (Romans 12:1).

A friend sent us a video from Rome. They had left Israel and traveled to Rome, finding the spot where Paul was martyred. Paul laid down his life for us, to teach us so much. In writing the book of Philippians, Paul told us how Jesus wanted us to live. He exhorted throughout Philippi that we lay down our lives so when people see us, they see Jesus. In setting aside our pride and instead giving all glory to the Lord, we are living witnesses to a life with Jesus in your heart.

Peace and Joy Day Ten

"For the Spirit God gave us does not make us timid, but gives us power, love and self-discipline" (2 Timothy 1:7).

We humans can get caught up in life, fearing, worrying, being defined by things and people we shouldn't allow into our lives. From 2 Timothy 1:7: "For the Spirit God gave us does not make us timid, but gives us power, love and self-discipline." By not living in fear, no one can define us; only God defines who we are. We forgive them with love, and self-control comes from His strength, not ours!

Peace and Joy Day Eleven

"But the fruit of the Spirit is love, joy, peace, forbearance, kindness, goodness, faithfulness" (Galatians 5:22).

Whatever you saturate your life with, you become. If you fill your life with confrontation, anger, always being right, and retaliation, your life will be filled with chaos. However, if instead you saturate your life with truth, kindness, gentleness, forgiveness, and godliness, you will continually grow to be more like our Lord.

Peace and Joy Day Twelve

"You will keep in perfect peace those whose minds are steadfast, because they trust in you" (Isaiah 26:3).

We wait in line at a store sale. We wait in line to see a concert. We wait in line to get into a ball game. We wait in line to get into a restaurant. So, why don't we wait on Jesus to give us His perfect will and more peace? I tried to gather all the grandchildren to have a worship service in our home last Sunday, but it was hard to pull them away from their technology. So, I mentioned that with all the time we give to everything else in our lives, this was our chance to give an hour to Jesus with no guilt, just a smile. They got the point and we communed together with the Lord. It was so special and filling! Let's give Him a little more time so He can give us more peace.

Peace and Joy
Day Thirteen

"Watch and pray so that you will not fall into temptation. The spirit is willing, but the flesh is weak" (Matthew 26:41).

Looking out my patio window I noticed several tiny birds. They were drinking out of the puddles from the rain and looking diligently for food. They seemed confident, but they had jerky movements with their bodies. I wondered how many people around me seem so confident but inside they are nervous. Often, we have all the confidence in what God is doing in our lives and that He is in control. However, our bodies can still feel the nervousness from the stress.

Dear Holy Spirit, come today and touch each one reading this with your peace, not only outwardly but deep within their souls. You are our comforter, our guide, and our hope. Touch all of us today we ask this in the name of the Father, the Son, and the Holy Spirit. Amen!

Peace and Joy
Day Fourteen

"In your relationships with one another, have the same mindset as Christ Jesus" (Philippians 2:5).

When I think of Jesus, here is what I see... His gentle but strong spirit, His unconditional love, His forgiveness to even those who hurt Him. He sat with those who weren't like Him. He stood for truth, even when the price seemed to be too high. The people close to Him betrayed Him, but He kept His eye on His purpose...loving His heavenly Father and fulfilling the plan so we can be with Him in heaven someday. He is our most loving and faithful friend. He is enough! I worship my Savior today! Join me sometime this morning in putting everything into His hands and putting on the mind of Christ. In Philippians 2:5 it says, "Your attitude should be the same as that of Christ Jesus!" We become what we saturate our lives in! I know it is hard, but if you think on Him and worship Him, He will fill you!

Peace and Joy Day Fifteen

"I am not saying this because I am in need, for I have learned to be content whatever the circumstances" (Philippians 4:11).

There is a reason for our deep need for peace. We were created to be in communion with God. With God in our heart and life, we operate from a place of peace. When in the midst of the storms that life can bring, we are able to have a peace that others won't be able to understand unless they know Jesus. The apostle Paul said, "Whatever state I find myself, therewith to be content!" It doesn't mean that we don't feel the stress of our circumstances. Instead, we can rest in God's care, knowing He can take care of all circumstances! Learning to rest and wait upon the Lord is hard, but choose Him today and you will have victory!

Peace and Joy
Day Sixteen

"Do not be anxious about anything, but in every situation, by prayer and petition, with thanksgiving, present your requests to God" (Philippians 4:6).

The book of Philippians is a joyful book—it mentions rejoice or joy sixteen times! Not happiness, which depends on happenings, but joy, which comes from Jesus. No matter what we face, we can remain steady in who we choose to live like. All this was taught by Paul as he sat in prison—yeah, that's correct, prison!

This peace is available to us, but He can't do it without us choosing his way and not ours! Jesus, with His supernatural powers, guide and deliver us from the things of this world into peace and joy! Amen.

PEACE AND JOY
DAY SEVENTEEN

"And the peace of God, which transcends all understanding, will guard your hearts and your minds in Christ Jesus" (Philippians S 4:7).

The Israelites were provided for and given their freedom. Sadly, they forgot who God was and that He was the source of both. Let's not forget who God is, and not only what He has done, but what He can do if we trust Him and do not waiver.

Tony Evans' new book called *God Himself* states that our Holy Father gives us the foundation of our beliefs.[1] We need to be reminded of this over and over again. So, if we know Him, we can have peace in Him.

PEACE AND JOY
DAY EIGHTEEN

"I can do all this through him who gives me strength" (Philippians 4:13).

Paul said that he learned to be content regardless of the situation. I just reminded myself of that when both cars had to be repaired at the same time. What do you need repaired? Whatever it is, don't let it rob you of your peace. Our friend Ralph McSwain said years ago, "If you have a problem, write it down and put it in a drawer. Close the drawer and open it a week later." When I remembered those words, I was able to take a deep breath, put my cars in the "drawer." The repairs were made, and again, Jesus showed me He will take care of all if I give Him control. Give the Lord control when trouble comes your way. Be content knowing He's got it!

Peace and Joy
Day Nineteen

"Therefore, if anyone is in Christ, the new creation has come: The old has gone, the new is here!" (2 Corinthians 5:17).

Too many times we are acting out who we think we are, when really, it's who we have become. I think that's why when people turn to Jesus, they call it being "Born Again." It's a new life for the person He sees and loves just the way they are. He just wants us to be our best self, but we have to choose Him in order for that to happen. This is advice for everyone. He gives us hope and molds our circumstances and us. Choose Jesus and begin a new life of true peace.

Peace and Joy
Day Twenty

"Do not be anxious about anything, but in every situation, by prayer and petition, with thanksgiving, present your requests to God" (Philippians 4:6).

I'm searching for a few things this morning. First, I'm searching for Spring—what happened to it? Second, I'm searching for a replacement for Mondays; why are we so tired on Mondays? Third, I'm searching for the fountain of youth! We had a short get-away this past weekend to Gatlinburg, Tennessee, and I have never been so tired upon returning from a vacation. We managed to pick the weekend of the largest classic car show in all of the United States! Thousands of classic cars, filling the streets. A snail could have beat us in a race:) Gatlinburg is one of our favorite places, and we have a few "must see/do" places each time we go. The gridlock caused by the car show was messing with our ability to move about. I started to get anxious in those moments, then I looked over at Tony, who was in heaven seeing all those cool cars, and reminded myself of all the people we'd already met. That little gut check confirmed we didn't have to hit all of the "must see/do." Jesus showed me that if I take a deep breath and have a little patience, a new experience can be a blast! Have a week with love and patience.

PEACE AND JOY
DAY TWENTY-ONE

"Whatever you have learned or received or heard from me, or seen in me—put it into practice. And the God of peace will be with you" (Philippians 4:9).

I learned this today... MOSES taught us to thank God for what we have. DAVID taught us to thank GOD even in the darkest valley! PAUL taught us to thank God in times of deep pain. Not for the pain, but for what the pain produces!

Then I realized—I've been learning these lessons over the last twenty-five years of living through life's experiences. Today God just revealed the connection of how these three men's lives were intertwined. Each desired to be more like the Holy of Holies, the one true God. I can't wait to see what else God will reveal to me in the next ten years and in what areas I will become more like Him.

PEACE AND JOY
DAY TWENTY-TWO

"My sheep listen to my voice; I know them, and they follow me" (John 10:27).

Rest in the presence of the Lord today! Watch for Him to show up in amazing ways! Look for Him in a bird, a cloud, or even in a quiet moment. Listen for His voice—it may come in a sermon; it may come from someone you love; it may come in a song. His options are infinite.

Watch, look, and listen for Him. Take our eyes off the noise of this world, Lord. We can be healed and comforted by You. So we give You our moments! Amen.

Peace and Joy
Day Twenty-Three

"The LORD makes firm the steps of the one who delights in him; though he may stumble, he will not fall, for the LORD upholds him with his hand" (Psalms 37:23–24).

Each day I ask the Holy Spirit what I need to post. I am not writing for the masses—I am writing for you! Today, I heard one word: "STEP." One step can take us backwards; one step in attitude, recurring sin, or even omitting something we should do. Then I realized that even one step of not being honest with ourselves can literally keep us from growing, learning, or changing! One simple moment not facing truth. WOW! This is why our connection with God protects us even from ourselves! One step forward can take us to God! I bow before the God that changes me—or not! It is always a step of choice!

Peace and Joy
Day Twenty-Four

"But now that you have been set free from sin and have become slaves of God, the benefit you reap leads to holiness, and the result is eternal life" (Romans 6:22).

A bond or bondage? That is the question you can ask yourself when making a major decision. The definition of the word bond is a force or a feeling that unites people; a common emotion and/or interest. The definition of bondage: a state of being a slave. Notice the difference when there's a bond it's freely chosen and enjoyed because of the common goals. But bondage—remember, a slave has no freedom. A slave is not respected, and a slave has no hope. Unless they fight for their freedom. Do not choose bondage. "Don't go someplace you don't want to stay." Let Jesus help you with all your decisions. Use His values and principles that He taught us in the New Testament to make your decisions. When you do you, you will find freedom and peace.

Peace and Joy
Day Twenty-Five

"In everything set them an example by doing what is good. In your teaching show integrity, seriousness" (Titus 2:7).

Three years ago, my friend Karen sold us her dad's very old Shopsmith saw. For those of you who don't know it beyond a saw, it also has a lathe and anything else you'd need to do woodworking. Tony has always wanted one! It's like sixty years old, but it is incredible. Tony has been able to help both of our grandsons make wood ballpoint pens. They absolutely loved it. This morning, he was watching someone using a Shopsmith on TV, and I said, "You should make something else with the boys. Maybe even if you just make some table legs to show them how.

Even if they don't know what they would attach them to, when you are gone someday you will have given them legs to stand on! Get it? He will have left them with life tools and memories of his time, talents, and love!

What are you leaving behind? We can't leave anything behind if we haven't filled our self-up with something to give. Fill your soul with Jesus, give His love away, and then fill yourself back up again with His Word.

PEACE AND JOY
DAY TWENTY-SIX

"For I am the Lord your God who takes hold of your right hand and says to you, Do not fear; I will help you" (Isaiah 41:13).

I saw a picture of just a tiny hand holding a mother's hand. I thought of baby Jesus, His little hand holding onto Mary. How humbled and honored and loving Mary must have felt that at moment in time. As now, as we hold on to His hand, His words, His miracles, His love. Rest in Him during this celebration of Him always.

PEACE AND JOY DAY TWENTY-SEVEN

"I have told you this so that my joy may be in you and that your joy may be complete" (John 15:11).

What makes you happy? I got this small carved black bear in Gatlinburg, our favorite place to vacation. Such wonderful memories. The bear is laying on its belly with its head laying on crossed paws in the front, hanging over the edge of a shelf in our guest bathroom. Just hanging out, looking over at me. I'll just take a minute, look at it, and smile every time. Think for a minute, what always makes you smile just looking at it? Joy doesn't have to be complex.

PEACE AND JOY DAY TWENTY-EIGHT

"But everything should be done in a fitting and orderly way" (1 Corinthians 14:40).

I set aside today to clean out the clutter in my closet. I needed to get stuff out of there and get the rest organized.

Then I felt like I heard this: Is there other clutter in my life that's keeping me from being as effective as I should be?

The first answer for me was—I'm eating too much sugar. Two years ago when faced with a hardship, I turned to sugar. At least that's my excuse. I'm asking the Lord to help me clean out any clutter in my heart and mind! You see, nothing is more important to me than His presence and power in my life. We just can't survive in this broken world without Him. What is the clutter in your life: negativity, too much busyness, or working too hard? Take a minute today and reflect, then take baby steps and clean out your clutter.

PEACE AND JOY DAY TWENTY-NINE

"Therefore I tell you, whatever you ask for in prayer, believe that you have received it, and it will be yours" (Mark 11:24).

Sometimes we lay our burdens at the foot of the Cross, but then we pick it back up. Don't waver in your faith, trust Him. Don't beg Him because it means you don't trust Him. Dear Jesus, we lay all of our burdens at Your feet and we trust You, amen.

PEACE AND JOY
DAY THIRTY

"His master replied, 'Well done, good and faithful servant! You have been faithful with a few things; I will put you in charge of many things. Come and share your master's happiness!'" (Matthew 25:21).

Before I was even a wife, I dreamed about what type of grandmother I would be! My husband assured me that was not normal. I loved going to both of my grandmother's homes, but there wasn't much to do in those days. Last night my granddaughter was telling me of memories that she had of different things we did together with "The COUSINS."

Mission accomplished but not finished yet! Can you imagine how our heavenly Father plans things for our lives? All we have to do is listen and obey! Someday when His story is complete in us, He will smile and say, "Well done, my faithful servant!" Bow before Him today and take time to listen. His story for you is beautiful.

Peace and Joy Day Thirty-One

"I praise you because I am fearfully and wonderfully made; your works are wonderful; I know that full well" (Psalms 139:14).

Lord, we thank You for the privilege of being Yours and serving You in this unique season of life! Whether we are old, young, sick, healthy, sad, or happy, You have loved us, allowing us to be where we are and who we are. May we walk in the peace of WHOSE we are! Amen.

PEACE AND JOY
DAY THIRTY- TWO

"Come to me, all you who are weary and burdened, and I will give you rest" (Matthew 11:28).

What are you focused on today? We have so many things that we have to think about, even the time we have for the weekend. Stop for a moment and take a deep breath and be thankful. Laugh about something. Let go of your opinions or plans and just rest your mind. Remember when Jesus took time away? I know He watched the birds and the sky and the mountain stream. At least in my mind, He did! I love Him so much; I think I will just think about His sweet, gentle love for me!

Peace and Joy Day Thirty- Three

"I press on toward the goal to win the prize for which God has called me heavenward in Christ Jesus" (Philippians 3:14).

For the first time in our married life, our Christmas decorations are down and put away before New Years. I'm ready to begin a new year. Putting everything behind me and continuing to press toward the story HE HAS WRITTEN.

No one and nothing matters more! Hold on to everything loosely, my friends so that the Holy Spirit can freely work in your lives! What do you need to put behind you in order to move forward?

PEACE AND JOY DAY THIRTY- FOUR

"Be strong and courageous. Do not be afraid or terrified because of them, for the LORD your God goes with you; he will never leave you nor forsake you. The LORD himself goes before you and will be with you; he will never leave you nor forsake you. Do not be afraid; do not be discouraged" (Deuteronomy 31:6–8).

Just a reminder to someone that needs reminding... the beauty of belonging to Jesus is that He is our hope. He never leaves us. He heals our hearts and minds and bodies. He gives us joy in the midst of the storms of life! Yes, you still feel it all, but you will never be without hope! His very character is hope in action. Trust Him!

Peace and Joy
Day Thirty- Five

"You will keep in perfect peace those whose minds are steadfast, because they trust in you" (Isaiah 26:3).

Friday...the day that we think about the week we just had. Friday...the day we look forward to because the weekend is almost here and our thoughts go to all we're going to do. What about enjoying just today! Sit with the Holy Spirit, take a deep breath, be thankful, and give the past to Him. Trust the future to Him. The peace that we all so want will come. Thank You, Jesus.

Peace and Joy
Day Thirty- Six

"Peace I leave with you; my peace I give you. I do not give to you as the world gives. Do not let your hearts be troubled and do not be afraid" (John 14:27).

When I think of Jesus, I smile or tear up. When we look away from what we see in these worlds of our flesh and look to Him, our hearts are lifted up. If you look to who He is, you'll see Him through His Word and through prayer. Trust who He is for you and for the ones you love. Listen to Him and not all the other voices in your life. Such wonderful peace will be yours.

PEACE AND JOY
DAY THIRTY- SEVEN

"Then he said to them all: 'Whoever wants to be my disciple must deny themselves and take up their cross daily and follow me. For whoever wants to save their life will lose it, but whoever loses their life for me will save it'" (Luke 9:23–24).

I woke up this morning surprised at a dream. I was in a room at a church working with about twenty young adults, Tony and me. After teaching the lesson, I asked them to take something of theirs and put it in a ziplock bag I was holding. I put in a small piece of food. Others put in a pen, a tiny piece of plastic furniture, a heart, multiple pieces of paper with something written on them and a clock...

...After I woke up, I thought how strange this was. I knew it was from the Lord, so I asked Him what it meant. He said everything in the bag represents something we can't die to. I knew why mine was food. I had gotten back to eating poorly and didn't feel well. I had asked the Lord to show me why

I felt so bad just before going to sleep that night. The pen represented the words we say to others, to ourselves, and to God. The tiny furniture piece was for every possession we hold dear. The heart was the things we worry about....

... The papers represent everything we hold within us that nobody knows about—things we carry around but don't have to. The clock stands for our time, used well or wasted. When the Holy Spirit revealed this to me, I had to write it down.

Paul wrote about dying to ourselves. He knew the less we have of ourselves, the more we have of Jesus. The more of His nature that lives within us, the more we can live a powerful life. God used a dream to teach me about food, relationships, possessions, and time. Keep them in a bag, then take them out only as He needs them to bless others or to help us grow closer to Him.

SUFFERING

Years ago, my pastor had a sermon that was titled, "I Don't Want This in My Life."

"I don't want this in my life!"

None of us want to suffer, but this can be a time when we draw closer to God like never before.

Second Corinthians 12:9 says, "But my grace (unearned favor) is sufficient for you, for my power is made perfect in weakness." The Holy Spirit was left for us by Jesus to give us comfort and guidance and peace in the midst of the storms of life!

SUFFERING DAY ONE

"He said: 'Listen, King Jehoshaphat and all who live in Judah and Jerusalem! This is what the Lord says to you: "Do not be afraid or discouraged because of this vast army. For the battle is not yours, but God's"'" (2 Chronicles 20:15).

The challenges ahead may seem like giants! As I typed that, I smiled... I spoke about that at our last retreat. My question was, "What are your giants?"

My giants seem big but so were David's! Our faith has to be bigger than our giants. The strength wasn't in the tiny stone, it was in David's belief that God could take care of anything He had asked David to do or face.

I have given that message twice in my life, and both times it impacted me as much as the group I spoke to! Dear sweet Holy Spirit, we believe in You as our comforter, guide, and the power in everything, so we lay all things at Your feet!

Prepare our hearts each day to walk in Your strength, not our own. We completely trust You! Amen.

SUFFERING DAY TWO

"And the God of all grace, who called you to his eternal glory in Christ, after you have suffered a little while, will himself restore you and make you strong, firm and steadfast" (1 Peter 5:10).

Suffering humbles us.
Suffering teaches us.
Suffering changes us.
Suffering brings us closer to His presence.
Suffering fills us with His joy.
Suffering enables us to represent His power to others.

SUFFERING DAY THREE

Finally, brothers and sisters, whatever is true, whatever is noble, whatever is right, whatever is pure, whatever is lovely, whatever is admirable—if anything is excellent or praiseworthy—think about such things. Whatever you have learned or received or heard from me, or seen in me—put it into practice. And the God of peace will be with you.) *(Philippians 4:8–9).*

I heard a paster say, "What we care about, we talk about!" During this difficult time of our lives for Tony and me, we have a lot to think, feel, and care about. For this to not overwhelm us, we do two things: we laugh and we talk about Jesus to each other and with our friends. When I heard this statement, I realized—Wow; thank You, Lord. We want to be saturated with You, not our flesh. Often when I've spoken to groups, I've said... whatever you saturate your life with, you become. Even when it feels like we have no choices, we always have the choice to worship Him. Sing those worship songs, talk to Him, read His Word; He will provide comfort, strength, and wisdom to weather your storm.

Suffering Day Four

"You will keep in perfect peace those whose minds are steadfast, because they trust in you" (Isaiah 26:3).

There are many people, each one different, reading this right now. Each of you are facing something different today and will tomorrow and the rest of the month.

Whatever it is, the God who created the heavens and the earth is personally in this with you. Willing to give you His power, His healing, His peace. The one thing each of us have in common is His availability to us through prayer. He's listening and is answering. Sometimes we may not feel or see His answer, but He always does. Choose Him, rest in Him, and have His peace, knowing God is in this for you and with you.

Suffering Day Five

"Do not conform to the pattern of this world, but be transformed by the renewing of your mind. Then you will be able to test and approve what God's will is—his good, pleasing and perfect will" (Romans 12:2).

We've entered a very difficult time in our world. That is why it's more important than ever that if we say we are Christian, we must be Christ-like. Maybe most of the time you probably are, but what about those times that you aren't?

What is it that keeps you living like Jesus?

As I have worked with so many people, I have become more and more convinced that a large portion of them do not realize that they need healing. When the need for healing becomes undeniable, folks often run instead of doing the work needed because it is scary, too difficult, or painful!

But now is the time to clear out those old negative tapes that play in your head and replace them with your love for Jesus! I am convinced that loving Him more than ourselves is the answer to becoming more like Him. Be courageous, start today!

Suffering Day Six

"Blessed are the pure in heart, for they will see God" (Matthew 5:8).

Something came to me during prayer early this morning; I hope I can communicate it effectively. Often, when we go through a horrible crisis in our lives, we have trouble trusting God.

I think the reason is because we have feelings that were a part of our mistakes when we walked in our flesh. But the Holy Spirit wants us to give up our part in this. I think we carry it because we think that's part of our punishment.

He wants us to let him have all of it: our mistakes, our regrets, our fears, and our thoughts of the future. Remember the vision of the broken window...He said, "You see me through your brokenness, but I see you clearly." Let Him have it, my friend—all of it, even your part of it, then you'll be able to live in peace.

Suffering Day Seven

"But those who hope in the LORD will renew their strength. They will soar on wings like eagles; they will run and not grow weary; they will walk and not be faint" (Isaiah 40:31).

Today the Holy Spirit reminded me again of how He works. This is often in unique ways, and often He takes more time than we think it should! He never fails, and He makes things better than we think. If you're facing impossible situations, ask to see life through His eyes. I just want to remind you that even if you think you know what the outcome will be, God does it bigger and better and more perfect. His outcome will be stronger than the pain that you are experiencing and the Holy Spirit, His comforter, will be with you while you wait.

Suffering Day Eight

"Let us examine our ways and test them, and let us return to the LORD" (Lamentations 3:40).

Have you ever talked with your spouse or a dear friend about your future? The Lord says we will have big hills and valleys on our earthly journey.

My husband and I recently had such a discussion. Despite some significant challenges looming in the future, I have been able to make him crack up laughing several times in the last forty-eight hours.

I like who he is, including his sense of humor, and I like who I am, even with my wacky sense of humor. Do you like who you are? Don't look into the mirror and evaluate your human form, but look through the window and see how the Lord, Jesus Christ, sees you in His eyes. His perspective will help you navigate your unique journey.

Suffering Day Nine

"So do not fear, for I am with you; do not be dismayed, for I am your God. I will strengthen you and help you; I will uphold you with my righteous right hand" (Isaiah 41:10).

As I felt the warmth of a tear flowing down my cheek, I remembered Paul in prison, Peter and his grief at denying Jesus, and the challenge of leading the church. I remember Daniel untouched in the lion's den, Moses suffering from old age but being asked and fulfilling His call. Then, I remember Jesus and how He made sure John would take care of His mother Mary after He was gone.

We serve a God of miracles, of love and power. Choose Him over all that you see and feel today. He will be with you wherever you are—all you need to do is ask!

Suffering Day Ten

"But those who hope in the LORD will renew their strength. They will soar on wings like eagles; they will run and not grow weary; they will walk and not be faint" (Isaiah 40:31).

I was sitting on my sofa, praying for someone who called last night. When I looked out of the windows at the gray, empty branches of the trees, suddenly an eagle flew through those trees, swirling in and out. It was breathtaking. I thought that when we are in the darkest times of our lives, unsure of what lies ahead, the Lord is like an eagle because He soars through our lives with hope! Take hope, my friends. Trust Him! "Those who wait upon the Lord will renew their strength, they will soar on wings like eagles, they will run and not grow weary, they will walk and not faint!"

Suffering Day Eleven

"If any of you lacks wisdom, you should ask God, who gives generously to all without finding fault, and it will be given to you" (James 1:5).

What's on your mind? Each of us lives in our own thoughts. That's why it's important when we go through something to discuss it with someone to get it out of our heads and put it into perspective. A lot of people just aren't good at that. If you are one of them, just pray. Ask the Holy Spirit to take you from the natural to the supernatural. In the book of James, it talks about asking Him for wisdom and He will give it to you. Remember, when Jesus went to rise up into heaven, He said, "I won't leave you comfortless. I will give you a comforter." Saturate your mind with His wisdom and you will find the path you need to take."

Suffering Day Twelve

"But whatever were gains to me I now consider loss for the sake of Christ" (Philippians 3:7).

Just a reminder... All of your losses are really gains. Why? A loss is a reminder that Satan is really afraid of your love for Jesus and is trying to get to you.

It is an opportunity for God to show you His power, mercy, grace, and love.

It is your opportunity to show others who God really is by living like Him in the supernatural instead of the natural (your flesh). I choose to turn to Him in every loss I experience. If Job of the Bible can trust and be content through his circumstances, if you come to the Lord in prayer, He will help you be content in whatever circumstances you encounter.

Suffering Day Thirteen

"But our citizenship is in heaven. And we eagerly await a Savior from there, the Lord Jesus Christ, who, by the power that enables him to bring everything under his control, will transform our lowly bodies so that they will be like his glorious body" (Philippians 3:20–21).

We worship You, our great and mighty God! We look beyond our sight to You and to Your love for us.

We look beyond the fact that there is not trust in what humans claim as truth, but You are truth and peace. We choose to sit in your arms, and as you hold us, we are healed and are given wisdom.

We know that our eternal home is in heaven with You and not here! Please open our eyes to Your glory and power. Give us peace!

We need only to touch the hem of Your garment, and then we will be fine!

Suffering Day Fourteen

"Be strong and courageous. Do not be afraid or terrified because of them, for the LORD your God goes with you; he will never leave you nor forsake you" (Deuteronomy 31:6).

You can feel fear, but don't be afraid. We're going to be afraid sometimes, but that doesn't mean we don't go forward anyway. Jesus gives us the strength, the wisdom, and the power to go forward, in spite of how we feel. Psalm 118. 6: "The Lord is on my side; I will not fear." We choose Him and not fear. We choose Him and not bitterness. We choose Him and we have joy.

Each day remember to be thankful for who He is in that we will have so much more to be thankful for. Hallelujah.

Suffering Day Fifteen

"You will keep in perfect peace those whose minds are steadfast, because they trust in you" (Isaiah 26:3).

As I sit on my sofa looking out the back window, all the branches are empty; it looks dreary. It seems that it was just yesterday the trees were full of leaves. Change isn't always pretty. It can be really dreary, but the leaves have to fall for a reason. Room must be made for new life and renewal. As you live through those moments of life that are so very painful and can be downright ugly, remember that Jesus takes ashes and turns them into beauty. Jesus is the only one that can give you peace in the middle of the storm because He is doing things you cannot do for yourself!

Suffering Day Sixteen

"May the God of hope fill you with all joy and peace as you trust in him, so that you may overflow with hope by the power of the Holy Spirit" (Romans 15:13).

This is my battle cry! Human nature surprises me often. I have a deep resolve to choose Jesus and joy. Yet, when we have days like yesterday was for me, we can hit a wall that alone we can't jump over or break through. Each of us has a human limit, but when we choose God's Spirit, He can make the way forward. I chose His supernatural over my natural. Someone so dear to me just received a scary diagnosis. It's going to be an ugly fight for them and their family. I'm choosing to let it go and instead live every minute just in love with Jesus, have joy and laughter no matter what! Nothing will limit my choice to be like Jesus! Peace, peace, wonderful peace flowing down from the Father above.

Suffering Day Seventeen

"Devote yourselves to prayer, being watchful and thankful" (Colossians 4:2).

Lord, we start this day with You! Thank You for Your great healing love.

Thank You for the path of life You have given us.

Not only for those You have brought our way that blessed us, but also for the times You have set us aside to draw us nearer to You! Amen.

Suffering Day Eighteen

"Return to your rest, my soul, for the LORD has been good to you" (Psalms 116:7).

Stop trying! Stop trying to make that relationship work, stop trying to solve all of those problems, and start Trusting!

Trust the One who can do all things. Trust the One who has the plan, but can only execute the plan if you will allow it. We have to change our will (what we want and what we think we need) to trust Jesus! He left us the Holy Spirit to comfort and guide us. Today, end the trying and disappointment and begin trusting so you can receive His peace!

Suffering Day Nineteen

"And we know that in all things God works for the good of those who love him, who have been called according to his purpose" (Romans 8:28).

Visited a church yesterday, and on each side of the platform were huge crosses. All during the service, my eyes were drawn to the crosses. I kept hearing, "He made it through that awful suffering because He knew why. He knew that it would all end up okay."

How was He so certain? It's because He knew His Father loved Him and was in charge. And then I thought, but we also know the Father is in charge of our lives. We also know the end is good. Not only heaven, but He always works things for our good.

Suffering Day Twenty

"For now we see only a reflection as in a mirror; then we shall see face to face. Now I know in part; then I shall know fully, even as I am fully known" (1 Corinthians 13:12).

Looking at the fog out my back window, where I usually see horses in the next yard, I can barely see the fence. And I was wondering, where are the horses?

Isn't that how we see? We can only see what's right in front of us. God knows what's beyond the fog, and the pain, and the fear, and even beyond the joy that we experience.

We can trust that Jesus sees and that He is our sight when we choose Him. Even if we don't see things clearly yet, we're squinting in the fog, peering through the mist. But it won't be long before the weather clears and the sun shines bright. We'll see it all clearly. We'll see it as God sees us, knowing Him directly, just as He sees us.

SUFFERING DAY TWENTY-ONE

"And the God of all grace, who called you to his eternal glory in Christ, after you have suffered a little while, will himself restore you and make you strong, firm and steadfast" (1 Peter 5:10).

I have had the privilege of speaking at women's conferences. One of my favorite presentations is about dealing with hardship/challenges. Some days the challenges ahead will seem like giants; as I typed that, I smiled. WHAT ARE YOUR GIANTS? My giants may seem or, in actuality, are big, and so were David's. Our faith has to be bigger than our giants. The strength wasn't in that tiny stone he threw, but in David's belief that God could take care of anything he had asked of David. Twice in my life the Lord has given me that message. Both times it impacted me as much as the group I was speaking to. Dear sweet Holy Spirit, we believe in You as our comforter, guide, and the power in everything. We lay all things at Your feet. Prepare our hearts each day to walk in your strength and not our own. We completely trust You! Amen.

Suffering Day Twenty-Two

"He will cover you with his feathers, and under his wings you will find refuge; His faithfulness will be your shield and rampart" (Psalm 91:4).

Psalm 91 is a chapter that you often hear people suggest that you read. In verse 4, it says, "His faithfulness will be your shield and rampart." Sometimes I look up definitions of words to see if there is a larger definition than the one that first comes to mind. One of the definitions of rampart is "a defensive and protective barrier."[2]

When His Holy Spirit enters our heart even in the midst of our flaws and distresses, He will be our protective barrier. So read Psalm 91 today and often to be reminded of how His great love protects you (Psalm 91:4).

Suffering Day Twenty-Three

"But as for me, I watch in hope for the LORD, I wait for God my Savior; my God will hear me" (Micah 7:7).

The sun of spring and summer brings lightness and hope to my heart. Winter, however, is just the opposite. Cold, dreary, naked trees. When the season changes our weather, trees drop off old leaves. When winter is over, trees bud new leaves and the beauty starts all over again. What season are you in? Are you willing to leave the old and take time to rest in Jesus to learn more about Him? We often feel like this is a time of waiting, and waiting is hard. But it's also a time of learning—learning how you handle stress and learning how to obey what He asks of you. Keep in your heart while you're waiting that God is working. You may not see it, but He is.

Suffering Day Twenty-Four

"For my thoughts are not your thoughts, neither are your ways my ways," declares the LORD. "As the heavens are higher than the earth, so are my ways higher than your ways and my thoughts than your thoughts" (Isaiah 55:8–9).

Something came to me during prayer this morning. Often when we go through a horrible crisis, we have trouble trusting God.

Trusting can be difficult because our thoughts will tell us that we were a part of causing it to happen. Even if that is true, you are forgetting Jesus' unconditional love.

He wants us to let Him have it all: our mistakes, our regrets, our fears, and our thoughts of the future. One day when praying, I thought of this great example. Picture a large broken window and on the other side of the window was the face of Jesus. But all we can see is the brokenness. Jesus, however, sees us clearly. Let Him have it, my friend, all of it, even if you were part of it, then you'll be able to live in peace.

SUFFERING DAY TWENTY-FIVE

"So David triumphed over the Philistine with a sling and a stone; without a sword in his hand, he struck down the Philistine and killed him" (1 Samuel 17:50).

There is no courage without danger. Sometimes we have to face danger head on in order to move on. When David faced Goliath, he didn't talk about how dangerous Goliath was—he talked about how great God is.

Don't talk fear. Talk faith.

SUFFERING DAY TWENTY-SIX

"I have told you these things, so that in me you may have peace. In this world you will have trouble. But take heart! I have overcome the world" (John 16:33).

We have had a week that has included every emotion that a human can feel. Blessed, sad, stress, pain, laughter, love, and loss. But with the power of the Holy Spirit, His presence did exactly what Jesus said...comforted us, which allowed us to rest in Him.

God's power is available to all of us in everything we face! He waits for us to seek Him.

We may not recognize it right away, but we will be amazed at what He does. Seek Him and He'll show up because He loves us like no other can!

Suffering Day Twenty-Seven

"This day I call the heavens and the earth as witnesses against you that I have set before you life and death, blessings and curses. Now choose life, so that you and your children may live" (Deuteronomy 30:19).

Our natural instinct is to think that suffering is something really awful, but suffering can break you or sift you

The definition of sifting is to isolate something that is more important or useful. In Deuteronomy 30:19, it tells us to choose today life or death, a curse or a blessing.

Each time I've gone through suffering or someone I love has, I always say, "I'll get through this, but Lord, show me what can come out of this and I will do it." Show me what You want me to see and what I need to learn during this time. Then go forward with the care for yourself physically and wait on Him to release His power in you through healing and learning more about your character and God's character.

His great love for us wants to comfort and guide us through anything that comes our way. Remember, when you are in the valley, the one thing about the valley is there is a mountain on each side. The valley is so much smaller that the mountains of joy are waiting for you.

Suffering Day Twenty-Eight

"Therefore, if anyone is in Christ, the new creation has come: The old has gone, the new is here!" (2 Corinthians 5:17).

Life-changing—is a term we all have used. What does this mean to you? So many times, there's something we need to change and we can't seem to get there. Making excuses to ourselves is the most common thing holding you back. The biggest detriment by far is that we forget God is our Maker and He can remake the things that need to be changed when we can't. When you feel like you've hit a wall and don't see any way over or around it, remember He is the wind beneath our wings, and He can lift us higher and stronger than anything or anyone else can. I often recite this: "I bow before the God that changes me." He is the lifter of my head and heart. Choose to let Him help you.

Suffering Day Twenty-Nine

"There is a time for everything, and a season for every activity under the heavens: a time to be born and a time to die, a time to plant and a time to uproot" (Ecclesiastes 3:1–2).

As I am now an older adult (have to keep reminding myself since I have never grown up), we have more wisdom. One of the things I like to share with my younger friends is that there are seasons of life and we can't resent them. We have to forgive others and ourselves in order to live in freedom! We have to learn from every experience, good or bad. All we have gone through in our lives, God has been there and provided us with new information that will help us go onto the next season. Embrace each season and then move forward with joy!

Suffering Day Thirty

"Heal me, LORD, and I will be healed; save me and I will be saved, for you are the one I praise" (Jeremiah17:14).

I woke up this morning thinking of two friends going through very difficult things.

Prayer is not only a gift to those we pray for but also for yourself.

It draws the presence of the Holy Spirit into your heart and your home.

The beauty of His presence is a fullness of life that most people waste time searching for in other ways! It's so simple; just sit with Him! Worship Him! Talk to Him!

Don't forget my saying... "There's only one thing better than a visitation of the Holy Spirit and that's another one!"

Suffering Day Thirty-One

"And the God of all grace, who called you to his eternal glory in Christ, after you have suffered a little while, will himself restore you and make you strong, firm and steadfast" (1 Peter 5:10).

Watching *Restoration Road* with Clint Harp on television. This episode talked about an old theater in Sandusky, Ohio, that was destroyed by a storm. The whole back of the theater was wiped out, but the storm stopped tearing it down when it got to a huge, beautiful chandelier.

It was like the chandelier said STOP! You're not destroying me!

I looked over at Tony and said, "This is like life, when things keep happening. If you look up, God says STOP—I'll make it all right."

He is our light, our chandelier, our protection, our peace, our joy.

He says, look up, my child, look up!

Choose to look up today, my friend.

PRAYER

Prayer is our lifeline to hope and peace and joy.

It connects us to a sweet communion with God. Sometimes we just don't feel like praying. Or sometimes we are just too distraught to think of the words. In those times, I just say His name, Jesus, over and over again.

I have a recipe for prayer I give to people all the time… worship, make your request known, and listen.

All those you can do while riding in your car or loading your dishwasher, or just sitting quietly in a room looking at a fireplace.

Prayer Day One

"'For my thoughts are not your thoughts, neither are your ways my ways,' declares the LORD. 'As the heavens are higher than the earth, so are my ways higher than your ways and my thoughts than your thoughts'" (Isaiah 55:8–9).

Have you heard the term *higher ground*? Do you know what that means? It means that whatever you are facing—criticism, discouragement, having a bad day, feeling hurt or angry, addiction, lives broken or lost—choose to pray. Do what Jesus did as He faced all of that! Even if it isn't fair or easy, stand in a place that is humble, kind, and pure! Jesus' power always defeats sin—in the end, truth will win! Wait for Him on higher ground, solid and safe, knowing He will make it right!

No one defines you! Nothing can take your joy unless you let them! Happiness is based on happenings that are always changing but joy, joy is grounded deep in your values! With Jesus, you can do all things, because He is enough!

Prayer Day Two

"My sheep listen to my voice; I know them, and they follow me" (John 10:27).

I woke up early this morning and had the most unusual thing happen. You should know I do not speak Spanish, but I heard in my head and heart this: "Como esta usted." I knew it as a greeting from the Holy Spirit. Tony speaks Spanish, so I asked him what it meant—"How are you?" I asked Tony to give me an appropriate reply in Spanish, "Gloria Dios," which means Glory to God! What a way to start a day. Tony and I both knew it was something He was saying more to us!

You see, He wants us to listen for His words to lead us. He really needed to get our attention today. What gets yours? The only thing better than a visitation of the Holy Spirit is another one!

Prayer Day Three

"But the fruit of the Spirit is love, joy, peace, forbearance, kindness, goodness, faithfulness" (Galatians 5:22).

Are you overwhelmed today? Are you in a hurry? Do you have a lot on your plate to do? Years ago we had a really full life and a lot of people in our lives. I had fifty calls in two days on my answering machine when it stopped accepting calls!

So one day my husband walked in the room, and he asked me very lovingly this question: "You know Jude, that long list of people in your life? When do I get to the top of the list?" That was about thirty-five years ago. Every day since then, I have made sure that he consciously knew when I did something for him and thought of him. Sometimes it was just stopping in the middle of the kitchen and looking him in the eyes and speaking to him. Who are you forgetting today? Maybe you're forgetting even yourself? I think that's why one of the fruits of the Spirit was self-control. Not a coincidence that it was last, because it's the hardest.

Ask the Holy Spirit to make you aware when your life is out of balance!

Prayer Day Four

"But the Advocate, the Holy Spirit, whom the Father will send in my name, will teach you all things and will remind you of everything I have said to you" (John 14:26).

In reading a devotional by Charles H. Spurgeon, he pointed out something that each of us needs to remember.[3] When we have those days that we feel the Holy Spirit's presence intensely, we commonly make requests for miracles we need in that moment. But it's also a time we can ask Him to speak to us about things that we need to improve. When you think of the word *relationship*, remember it involves two. Speak to Him, but also have an open heart to listen for His guidance.

Prayer Day Five

"Wait for the Lord; be strong and take heart and wait for the Lord" (Psalm 27:14).

Sometimes we have to just stop thinking about everything in our lives; just bundle it all up and lay it at the feet of Jesus. Ask Him to take care of it all, then comes the hard part—wait and listen for His guidance and wisdom. You won't be disappointed (Psalm 27:14).

Prayer Day Six

"And without faith it is impossible to please God, because anyone who comes to him must believe that he exists and that he rewards those who earnestly seek him" (Hebrews 11:6).

My favorite book is *REACHING OUT* by Henry Nouwen.[4] The subtitle says "The Three Movements of the Spiritual Life." First is the movement from loneliness to solitude. Second is the movement of hostility to hospitality.

The final movement he tells us is that prayer undergirds everything; it's the foundation that makes possible the other two and is the core of spiritual life. Our communion with the Holy Spirit draws us near to the heart of God and empowers us to do all other things.

Prayer Day Seven

"Walk in obedience to all that the LORD your God has commanded you, so that you may live and prosper and prolong your days in the land that you will possess" (Deuteronomy 5:33).

Today the phrase "one step" came to me as I was praying. Then suddenly I knew. One step can take us backwards. One step in an attitude, recurring sin, or even omitting something we should do. Then, I realized that even one step of not being honest with ourselves can literally keep us from growing, learning, or changing. One simple moment not facing truth. WOW! This is why our connection with God protects us, even from ourselves! One step forward can take us to God! I bow before the God that changes me—or not! It's always a step of choice—a famous line from *Raiders of the Lost Ark*, "choose wisely"!

PRAYER DAY EIGHT

"Do not be anxious about anything, but in every situation, by prayer and petition, with thanksgiving, present your requests to God" (Philippians 4:6).

The book of Philippians is a joyful book, it mentions rejoice or joy sixteen times! Not happiness which depends on happenings, but joy which comes from Jesus. No matter what we face we can remain steady in who we choose to live like...Jesus and His supernatural powers and guidance deliver us from the things of this world into peace and joy! All this was taught by Paul as he sat in prison—yeah, that's correct, prison! This peace is available to us but He can't do it without us choosing His way and not ours!

Prayer Day Nine

"If any of you lacks wisdom, you should ask God, who gives generously to all without finding fault, and it will be given to you" (James 1:5).

What is one thing you need to do this day, tomorrow, or this year? Not a resolution that is easily tossed aside, but a commitment to create a better you.

No better time to start than now. It's hard to make a commitment when you don't have a solid foundation to stand on. He is the foundation of unconditional love and faithfulness. James 1:5 tells us, "If any of you lacks wisdom ask God, who gives generously to all without fault and it will be given to you." Go to the Lord in prayer and ask Him to give you wisdom, then listen.

PRAYER DAY TEN

"But seek first his kingdom and his righteousness, and all these things will be given to you as well" (Matthew 6:33).

As the day ends, look back; what do you see? What really mattered? Regrets—laundry, bills, car pool, soccer, or gymnastics? Maybe it was the smile of recognition as a child entered the room. Maybe it was calling an older parent.

Maybe it was giving grace, forgiveness, laughter, or telling someone you would pray for them. What do you see? Start the day with Jesus—even if it's in the car or on the job. He wants to make your day more beautiful!

Prayer Day Eleven

"Therefore I urge you to imitate me" (1 Corinthians 4:16).

I always choose to learn from life's circumstances. Today, I had to be reminded of things I've learned before. 1. A thankful heart is a heart that can get through anything (just breathe, Jude)! 2. All I will ever need is Jesus! 3. His love alone brings us peace in the storm (rest in Him)! 4. The prayers of God's people can be felt in the room and His strength given! I love You, Jesus!

Prayer Day Twelve

"May the God of hope fill you with all joy and peace as you trust in him, so that you may overflow with hope by the power of the Holy Spirit" (Romans 15:13).

This is my battle cry! Human nature surprises me often. I have a deep resolve to choose Jesus and joy. Yet, when we have days like yesterday was for me, we can hit a wall that alone we can't jump over or break through. Each of us has a humanly limit, but when we choose God's Spirit, He can make the way forward. I chose His supernatural over my natural. Yes, Tony's cancer is back; it's going to be an ugly fight. I'm choosing to let it go and instead live every minute just in love with Jesus, have joy and laughter no matter what! Nothing will limit my choice to be like Jesus! Peace, peace, wonderful peace flowing down from the Father above.

Prayer Day Thirteen

"Trust in the LORD with all your heart and lean not on your own understanding; in all your ways submit to him, and he will make your paths straight" (Proverbs 3:5–6).

"Trust in the Lord with all of your heart and lean not upon your own understanding. In all your ways acknowledge him and he will direct your path." Lord, help us to search our hearts so nothing stands between us and your complete power to work for us and protect us in this messed up world. I pray for those who need encouragement, healing, wisdom, and strength. We ask this in Jesus' name. AMEN!

Prayer Day Fourteen

"Command and teach these things. Don't let anyone look down on you because you are young, but set an example for the believers in speech, in conduct, in love, in faith and in purity" (1 Timothy 4:11–12).

Are you burdened down by your daily guilt, disappointments, unfulfilled dreams, and weaknesses? I watched my grandchildren overnight; looked into their eyes and hearts and saw an empty slate of life that we are writing on. Teach love, wisdom, courage, and love for Jesus! Look around—there are many around you ready to learn from your life. Make it all count by giving away your wisdom, newly reclaimed joy, and yes—even your failures. Change comes when we walk away from ourselves into others' lives. Jesus changes us to not only a life of peace but a life of purpose. Praying for your new vision and purpose.

Prayer Day Fifteen

"He says, Be still, and know that I am God; I will be exalted among the nations, I will be exalted in the earth" (Psalms 46:10).

"Finding such joy in looking at our Christmas tree. It is so beautiful! When our girls were little, we would turn off the room's lights and lay under the tree and I would read to them. Simple moments in life made everything easier! Forget Instagram, Pinterest, Facebook and your phone's camera. Instead, just be. Be present and enjoy those small moments! Rest for the soul is often found in quiet, uncomplicated places!

Prayer Day Sixteen

"Are not two sparrows sold for a penny? Yet not one of them will fall to the ground outside your father's care. And even the very hairs of your head are all numbered. So don't be afraid; you are worth more than many sparrows" (Matthew 10:29–31).

God uses broken things. It takes broken soil to produce a crop, broken clouds to give rain, broken grain to give bread, broken bread to give strength. It is the broken alabaster box that gives forth perfume. It is Peter weeping bitterly that returns in greater power than ever. It is the broken body of Christ that will not settle for anything other than His house being a house of prayer. How can you offer your brokenness to be used by God?

Prayer Day Seventeen

"Do not be anxious about anything, but in every situation, by prayer and petition, with thanksgiving, present your requests to God" (Philippians 4:6).

Paul tells us to pray instead of worrying. It's like that old saying, "It's easier to say than do." When you love someone, you wouldn't do anything to hurt the relationship. The last few years I felt like God was saying that when I worry, it shows that I don't really trust Him, which hurts my relationship with Him. Moms, we have a hard time with this. After all, for years we spent 24/7 taking care of and guiding little human being(s). Then, one day, they are grown and we have to release them, not only physically but spiritually as well. That's when you do what Paul says to "die daily" to yourself. Recognize and respect their personhood by holding your tongue.

Ask them if they would like your thoughts before you give them, and try not to take it personally when they disagree with you or choose a different course of action. Tell God what you feel; then let Him take care of the outcome, knowing that His love for them is even greater than yours. This last year we have practiced that more intensely than ever. Not worrying equals peace. I pray for the peace of your hearts every day.

Prayer Day Eighteen

"May these words of my mouth and this meditation of my heart be pleasing in your sight, LORD, my Rock and my Redeemer" (Psalms 19:14).

Often when I'm counseling a young person, parent, spouse, or friend, I have to remind them that talking badly about someone else results in making them look bad and not the person they are talking about. It's harder for adults to realize this because sometimes we feel justified in where we stand. Especially as Christians, we must be very careful with our words! Our very title, Christian, means we represent Him! "Let the words of my mouth and the meditation of my heart be heart be acceptable in thy sight; oh Lord, my strength and my salvation!" Our words of kindness become easier when our hearts are truly all His and in tune with Him. Our flesh, then, isn't as important!

Prayer Day Nineteen

"Commit your way to the Lord; trust in him and he will do this" (Psalms 37:5).

Lord, I give You this day. I trust You, no matter what this has for me. I will face it with strength, courage, joy, laughter, and peace because of who You are, not because of me. You're never failing, always loving, and ready to give me the wisdom and courage I need. You, Lord, You are my first love, and as long as I keep You first in all my decisions, my family and I will be victors!

Prayer Day Twenty

"For where your treasure is, there your heart will be also" (Matthew 6:21).

When awarding the Medal of Honor, the President used the term "larger than life" in speaking of this soldier. It made me think about how large life can be. We just have to be bigger than the circumstances in this demanding life. How? It really comes from our resolve to do what is right regardless of the cost—also known as integrity! Matthew says, "Where your treasure is, there your heart will be also." It is so much easier to make a courageous choice when your mind has chosen what or who you treasure most. This is why I call my Christian walk a love affair with Jesus. I love Jesus and will never purposely do anything to hurt Him or to misrepresent Him. Doesn't mean I don't make mistakes, but it's never intentional. I've set my mind that Jesus is my one true love. Every great decision that requires courage, I judge it by who He is, not who I am. The Bible says that "a double-minded" man cannot be this way. A single-minded man is the one whose guide is righteousness. We will never be perfect like our Savior, but it can always and should be our goal. It helps keep the tough days not so messy. What does He give? Life more abundant.

Prayer Day Twenty-One

"Therefore put on the full armor of God, so that when the day of evil comes, you may be able to stand your ground, and after you have done everything, to stand" (Ephesians 6:13).

Put on your armor of God, choose His sweet Spirit, love those that hurt you, give grace when it is unearned! Ask the Holy Spirit to give you His hope and dreams. Lay your head on the one that is the lifter of your head—then SOAR! Praying for so many of you!

PRAYER DAY TWENTY-TWO

"But seek first his kingdom and his righteousness, and all these things will be given to you as well" (Matthew 6:33).

My life scripture is: "Seek ye first the kingdom and His righteousness and all these things were added to you" (Matthew 6:33). As I've walked the journey of my life, I've tried to do just that. Today, as I was praying for so many of you, I suddenly saw a long, narrow path with a round, white entrance. Immediately, I remembered a description in Matthew 7:14: "But small is the gate and narrow is the road that leads to life and only few will find it." Seek the narrow path to know and follow him and let him take care of your life.

Prayer Day Twenty-Three

"He says, 'Be still, and know that I am God; I will be exalted among the nations, I will be exalted in the earth'" (Psalms 46:10).

Stop, look, listen! Stop and worship. Look for the Holy Spirit to show up in amazing ways and listen for His voice. Maybe even in another person's voice! If you give Him this time, He always shows up. I bow before the one that changes me.

Prayer Day Twenty-Four

"As long as it is day, we must do the works of him who sent me. Night is coming, when no one can work" (John 9:4).

I kept saying to my daughter, as she was growing up, instant gratification, or delayed gratification. Often, we put things off because we just don't feel like doing it at the moment.

That is what we do with prayer and Bible reading. On the back of a promise slip from my mom's promise box, there was this little poem... Satan temps us to shorten prayer. Satan temps us to postpone prayer. Satan temps us to omit prayer.

If we would just connect with the Lord, give Him a little bit of time. It will change our whole day. Yes, you may still have some trials but you have the strength to go through them. Find a way to make it work so that it doesn't get left out.

Often when I'm counseling a young person, parent,

spouse, or a friend, I have to remind them that talking bad about someone else results in making them look bad and not the person they are talking about. It's harder for adults to realize this because sometimes we feel justified in where we stand.

Especially as Christians we must be very careful with our words! Our very title Christian means we represent Him! "Let the words of my mouth and the meditation of my heart be heart be acceptable in thy sight; oh lord my strength and my salvation!" Our words of kindness become easier when our hearts are truly all His and in tune with Him. Our flesh then isn't as important!

Prayer Day Twenty-Five

"After Job had prayed for his friends, the LORD restored his fortunes and gave him twice as much as he had before" (Job 42:10).

After Job prayed for his friends, the Lord made him more prosperous and gave him twice as much as before.

The Lord blessed the latter part of Job's life more than the first.

Prayer is our visit with God and His visit with us.

Prayer is how we know Him more and a gift not only to those we pray for but also for ourselves.

Let's pray for each other, our country, for wisdom and to recognize the purpose He has for our lives.

Cut out a time this weekend to sit with Him, talk to Him and then listen for that soft voice, that whisper as He speaks to you.

Prayer Day Twenty-Six

"Teach us to number our days, that we may gain a heart of wisdom" (Psalms 90:12).

What is it that you need to rise up and just do? I have several things. Not putting time aside for something/someone, or not feeling like doing or thinking through anything; we all have really valid excuses. But what does God want?

Recently, I started putting time aside every day to do what He's asked, which was to finish a book I started a long time ago. What is yours?

Dear Lord, we give You this day and every day. Help us to see it all through Your eyes and with Your strength to push forward and push above circumstances that keep us from doing what You've called us to do.

Thank You for Your unconditional love, Lord. Amen.

FORGIVENESS

I love you,

Are three important words.

More important are three other words…i forgive you!

These must be action words too.

Words are often easy, but to make them really effective we must also put action behind them.

Remember that old saying, "actions speak louder than words"?

But love usually comes easier most of the time. To act out forgiveness is really difficult. You just have to act it. Our and your emotions will catch up later.

Jesus gave us forgiveness, so we must forgive others. We don't forget. So, try loving jesus so much today that you can act like him by forgiving someone.

Maybe that someone is yourself.

Forgiveness Day One

"Then Peter came to Jesus and asked, 'Lord, how many times shall I forgive my brother or sister who sins against me? Up to seven times?' Jesus answered, 'I tell you, not seven times, but seventy-seven times'" (Matthew 18: 21–22).

Just recently, I had to forgive someone for the third time. In my flesh, I would've just stayed away from that person from here on. I know Jesus wouldn't stay away from anyone and we're supposed to be like Him, so I asked Him to show me how to forgive. This is what I felt He taught me: You can still stay connected with someone and live like Jesus in front of them without being in their lives all the time. When you think of them, pray, then act our forgiveness. Eventually your emotions will catch up.

Forgiveness Day Two

"Do not judge, and you will not be judged. Do not condemn, and you will not be condemned. Forgive, and you will be forgiven" (Luke 6:37).

How can we expect to walk in freedom when we don't walk in forgiveness?

Are you a forgiving type of person? For some it comes naturally, for others it has to be a conscious choice. Regardless, in our humanness, we all reach a limit where our forgiveness well runs dry. The idiom "that's the straw that broke the camel's back" aptly describes when our brain tells us *enough*! I'm always the one that forgives. It isn't fair and I'm tired of it. Difficult as it will be, remember that Jesus' unconditional love forgives us time after time and then even more. You are right, it's not fair, but then neither was the cross He bared for us. When you reach that limit, take a deep breath and say to yourself, my heart belongs to Jesus and He knows what wrongs have been done. He will deal with those in His time and way. Our job is to show that unconditional love and to forgive, even if it isn't deserved. It's a gift you give yourself. Don't let pent up anger disrupt your peace.

Forgiveness Day Three

"Bear with each other and forgive one another if any of you has a grievance against someone. Forgive as the Lord forgave you" (Colossians 3:13).

Remember when you are in the valley you can stay there where the floods can gather, but look up—the view is good...of heaven!

Paying attention to where your eyes are looking is how you live. Just recently, my view of life started to overwhelm me. I realized I was letting it. I knew I needed to realize what you can't control. Give the pain of hurt to Him, and then let Him hold you.

When the struggle involves family or others dear to you, it will be harder because the pain will be more personal. Stepping aside to let God be God will be definitely hard but not impossible.

Start by praying to forgive them. By doing so, we are being obedient to God's laws. Forgiving doesn't mean the hurt magically disappears. In fact, we will probably have to wait for our emotions to catch up. Friend, be obedient, and then watch how He works.

Our view is Him! His power, His peace, His wisdom. Fix our gaze/view, our identity on Him and no one else!

Forgiveness Day Four

"As evening approached, the disciples came to him and said, 'This is a remote place, and it's already getting late. Send the crowds away, so they can go to the villages and buy themselves some food'" (Matthew 14:15).

I recently spoke about forgiveness. Forgiveness is a gift you give yourself to let go of so you can feel freedom and peace. When you forgive, it doesn't mean you excuse or condone what someone has done. It means that you have chosen the heart and mind of Christ for your own life.

When we mistreat anyone for any reason, we are not living like Jesus. Jesus even forgave His abusers. No one is justified in getting back at anyone, hurting anyone, making someone's life difficult. That is not the humility and beauty of a life in Christ. The Word says, "We must forgive to be forgiven."

No matter how you justify your actions, if you say you are a Christian, you must hold it up as a reflection of who Jesus is. You may still have feelings, but you choose different actions. When you do, your feelings will eventually follow.

Forgiveness Day Five

"But the fruit of the Spirit is love, joy, peace, forbearance, kindness, goodness, faithfulness" (Galatians 5:22).

Remember when Jesus stood before Pilate? He was humble, gentle, and loving, even though He already knew His fate. Ultimately, Jesus asked God to forgive those who persecuted Him. He chose to have mercy though not deserved, which is the definition of unconditional love.

Forgiveness Day Six

"Finally, brothers and sisters, whatever is true, whatever is noble, whatever is right, whatever is pure, whatever is lovely, whatever is admirable—if anything is excellent or praiseworthy—think about such things" (Philippians 4:8).

In the difficult world we live in, we see all kinds of things that are not as God intended.

Not being mean but being kind. Not making you feel guilty, but loved. Not living afraid but empowered. Not being religious but having a relationship with God.

Choose to truly care about someone's personhood. These things are what make a difference—one life at a time. If we live our lives as Jesus lived, our hearts will change. These choices are conditions of the heart! We have to allow our hearts to be changed.

Forgiveness Day Seven

"May the God of hope fill you with all joy and peace as you trust in him, so that you may overflow with hope by the power of the Holy Spirit" (Romans 15:13).

With each new day, each new week, each new weekend, we only have one choice for our lives that can bring us the fulfillment of the love, joy, and peace we need...JESUS! Our world CANNOT give us something it does not have! When I talk about forgiveness, I say, "Don't expect healing from the one who hurt you." So don't expect to be filled up by an empty world. He came here to show us in the flesh that He IS ENOUGH! As the weekend, holidays, or other stressors come, our days are filled with disappointment if we forget the solid rock we stand on: JESUS! Give Him some moments to fill you.

Forgiveness Day Eight

"And I tell you that you are Peter, and on this rock, I will build my church, and the gates of Hades will not overcome it" (Matthew 16:18).

God uses broken things. It takes broken soil to produce a crop, broken clouds to give rain, broken grain to give bread, broken bread to give strength. It is the broken alabaster box that gives forth perfume. It is Peter weeping bitterly after he denied Christ three times, and yet God used Peter upon which to build His church. It is the broken body of Christ that will not settle for anything other than His house being a house of prayer. How can we be His house if we aren't characterized by a culture of prayer, bless are the poor in spirit for theirs is a kingdom of God.

Forgiveness Day Nine

"Have mercy on me, O God, according to your unfailing love; according to your great compassion blot out my transgressions. Wash away all my iniquity and cleanse me from my sin" (Psalms 51:1–2).

Forgiveness is not only about forgiving others, sometimes we need to forgive ourselves, and that can be even more difficult. Satan doesn't want us to have peace. He wants us discouraged, empty, frustrated, and confused. God paid the price for all of our sins, including yours, with His death on the Cross. His forgiveness is complete and eternal. In moments when you feel Satan's influence, remember that Jesus' blood covers you. He gives you the peace/warmth of a Father's love. When you choose to accept God's love and, in turn, extend that love to others, peace will follow.

Forgiveness Day Ten

"Let your conversation be always full of grace, seasoned with salt, so that you may know how to answer everyone" (Colossians 4:13).

I recently spoke about forgiveness. Forgiveness is a gift you give yourself to let go and feel freedom and peace. When you forgive it doesn't mean you excuse or condone what someone has done or that you forget it. However, it does mean that you have chosen the heart and mind of Christ for your own life. When we mistreat anyone for any reason we are not living like Jesus. Jesus even forgave His abusers. No one is justified in getting back at anyone, hurting anyone, making someone's life difficult. That is not the humility and beauty of a life in Christ. The Word says, "We must forgive to be forgiven!" No matter how you justify your actions if you say you are a Christian, you must hold it up in a reflection of who Jesus is. You may still have feelings, but when you choose different actions, the feelings will eventually follow. Praying for so many of you.

Forgiveness Day Eleven

"Those who live according to the flesh have their minds set on what the flesh desires; but those who live in accordance with the Spirit have their minds set on what the Spirit desires. The mind governed by the flesh is death, but the mind governed by the Spirit is life and peace" (Romans 8:5–6).

I start this day… Because I can. I am alive and well. I start this week... my top priority is to live for Jesus. I start this week... I choose to live above my flesh. No matter what all things look like. I start this week looking at others from the view of the Cross. Jesus forgave the soldiers and the others on their Cross, relinquished His mother to John's care.

To forgive is a gift to yourself. Letting go of family into God's care is hard, but let's let God be God! I start this week...to pray, because to pray is to know God

Forgiveness Day Twelve

"For if you forgive other people when they sin against you, your heavenly Father will also forgive you" (Matthew 6:14).

Early this morning, I was talking to someone about forgiveness. I said, the person you need to forgive is more than just the pain they caused you in this life; not forgiving creates a broken heart.

When Jesus has your heart, you will be able to forgive; only He has the power to put us back together. Keep turning to Him and leaning on His wisdom and protection. Ask Him to heal your heart and theirs. I choose, He gives.

FORGIVENESS DAY THIRTEEN

"I sought the LORD, and he answered me; he delivered me from all my fears (Psalms 34:4).

One of the results of unforgiveness is fear. Fear that someone will hurt us again. Fear of judgment by others that someone will think we were wrong and they were not. The opposite of fear is forgiveness. Let go and give your fears in prayer to the Lord; His love will protect you. It's really hard for people to criticize a gentle, laughing spirit. When all those thoughts keep coming into your mind, choose to be like Jesus instead of reacting. Let Him take care of the rest.

Forgiveness Day Fourteen

"A new command I give you: Love one another. As I have loved you, so you must love one another" (John 13:34).

When an event happens in someone's life that hurts so deeply, it's hard to think of forgiving those involved. Each of us struggles with forgiveness because we think it's letting the other person off the hook for their actions. We need to remember that by forgiving, we open up more space in our mind and soul for creativity and joy! By not letting the abuse of that relationship keep going, even when those involved mean so much to us, this is a time we can realize our deepest desire is our first love—Jesus. The more we love Him, the more we have Him in our heart, the more we want to be like Him, our life becomes easier. He will take the chaos and replace it with His peace.

Forgiveness Day Fifteen

"And we know that in all things God works for the good of those who love him, who have been called according to his purpose" (Romans 8:28).

Unforgiveness comes in all forms. Not forgiving someone else. Not forgiving God. Not forgiving yourself. All of it results in chaos, turmoil, and the loss of your peace. So, go to the place you can trust, God! He always forgives us. When He is in control, whatever happens or doesn't happen is part of the story He wrote for you, and since the Bible tells us that "All things work together for good for those who love the Lord," you can trust that whatever is going on will work out for your benefit in the end.

Forgiveness Day Sixteen

"I, even I, am he who blots out your transgressions, for my own sake, and remembers your sins no more" (Isaiah 43:25).

Some days we just have to forgive not only others, but we often need to forgive ourselves. Satan likes to replay old movies! He wants us discouraged, empty, frustrated, and confused.

Remnember, God loves you unconditionally. For the sins of our past, He has already given forgiveness. He doesn't even remember them. So, we don't have to keep begging for forgiveness; it was done on the Cross. So, choose peace over old movies; accept His love for you and then extend that kind of love to everyone else. It's a gift you give yourself.

Forgiveness
Day Seventeen

"And when you stand praying, if you hold anything against anyone, forgive them, so that your Father in heaven may forgive you your sins" (Mark 11:25).

Is your heart heavy today? You may or may not know why. Sit down and ask the Holy Spirit to reveal it to you and how to eliminate your heavy heart. It may be that you need to forgive someone. What if they haven't asked for your forgiveness? The Word says in Matthew 6:15, "If you do not forgive others their sins, your father will not forgive your sins." Build your life on a solid foundation of forgiveness, peace, and mercy.

FORGIVENESS DAY EIGHTEEN

"If my people, who are called by my name, will humble themselves and pray and seek my face and turn from their wicked ways, then I will hear from heaven, and I will forgive their sin and will heal their land. Now my eyes will be open and my ears attentive to the prayers offered in this place" (2 Chronicles 7:14–15).

As our world begins to go back to normal a little at a time, help us to not forget the things we have learned. Help those who have been so wounded in their hearts by all this. Heal those who are angry to change their anger into helping others each day. Feed the hungry, the abandoned, and those who feel loss, and give understanding to those who don't understand their journey in life. We love You, Lord, and so we choose to go beyond our feelings and focus on Your love. We trust You to lead us into the path of peace.

Forgiveness
Day Nineteen

"Finally, brothers and sisters, whatever is true, whatever is noble, whatever is right, whatever is pure, whatever is lovely, whatever is admirable—if anything is excellent or praiseworthy—think about such things" (Philippians 4:8).

"But the fruit of the Spirit is love, joy, peace, forbearance, kindness, goodness, faithfulness" (Galatians 5:22)

Forgiveness is one of our most important contributions to the healing of our world.

Someone who forgives and loves unconditionally and is willing to talk to even those we disagree with and treat them with unconditional love will change, if not the whole world, at least your world.

It will create such peace deep within your soul that it will affect every day that you live. As you've noticed, I often quoted Philippians 4:8 and Galatians 5:22.

The fruit of the Spirit will give you such a wonderful

guidance for your daily lives.

When you read them, look and see it really is coming from only a peaceful heart.

Read them today. I often check them periodically to check my own heart.

FINAL THOUGHTS

Yes, we're hearing about the end times and I believe they have begun. We'll hear about all the things that are going to happen and warnings to get prepared.

Don't forget—Jesus is coming back—things are going to be wonderful with Him. We will never be sick again. We will never be in need of anything ever again other than His presence.

How wonderful is that! Hallelujah! I wanted you to have some joy in the midst of a troubled world. Jesus loves you. He's always with you. He will always forgive you. He will always guide you because you love Him. He will always be enough; he will always be everything you need. Walk with Him through all of your days. *If you choose, ... He will give you blessings beyond your imagination.*

Please know, having this devotional in your possession is no accident. Tony, my "team," and I have prayed for each of you. May your life be supported and faith enriched by its contents. God chose to connect us, but you had to choose Him first! Continue to choose Him daily.

I choose, He Gives!

Acknowledgments

What do you get when you combine a functional nutrition therapist, oncology nurse, Christian counselor, financial client manager, data scientist, educator, actuary, surgical nurse, treasured neighbor, an owner of a travel agency, and a handsome and brilliant husband?

Answer:

TEAM JUDE!

This devotional has been my dream for over a decade. Thanks to this amazing group of godly people, it's become a reality.

Thank you all from the bottom of my heart.

- Meghan Adamo: Photographer, graphic designer
- Debbie Belshaw: FNTP
- Madeline DeGennaro: Oncology Nurse
- Joann Koenig: Nurse and Treasured Neighbor
- John Leslie: Managing Director Business Relationships
- Doug McKinley: Data Scientist
- Karen McKinley: Educator
- Shawn Parks: Consulting Actuary

- Beau Rootring: Christian Counselor
- Diane Smith: Nurse Manager Same Day Surgery (BSN, RN, CAPA)
- Lisa Vermaak: Owner of Blu Skyy Travel

TONY: At a church teen meeting, in the summer of my fifteenth year, I met a shy, but cute guy. That guy turned out to be the love of my life; my husband of fifty-seven years... Tony Way

Dearest Tony,

My journey could never have been this rich or entertaining without you by my side.

All my love,

Jude

ENDNOTES

1 Evans, Tony. 2020. *God, Himself.* Moody Publishers.

2 *Rampart.* n.d. In *Oxford Languages.* Accessed October 28, 2024. Oxford Languages-https://languages.oup.com/google-dictionary-en/.

3 Spurgeon, C H. 1996. *Holy Spirit Power.* New Kensington, Pa: Whitaker House.

4 Nouwen, Henri J. M. 1986. *Reaching out: The Three Movements of the Spiritual Life.* Garden City, N.Y. Image Books.

www.ingramcontent.com/pod-product-compliance
Lightning Source LLC
LaVergne TN
LVHW020946090125
800838LV00006B/89